Eezy Peezy Classical Favourites

WISE PUBLICATIONS
part of The Music Sales Group

London/New York/Paris/Sydney/Copenhagen/Berlin/Madrid/Tokyo

Published by

Wise Publications
14-15 Berners Street, London W1T 3LJ, UK.

Exclusive Distributors:

Music Sales Limited
Distribution Centre, Newmarket Road,
Bury St Edmunds, Suffolk IP33 3YB, UK.

Music Sales Corporation
257 Park Avenue South, New York, NY10010,
United States of America.

Music Sales Pty Limited
120 Rothschild Avenue, Rosebery,
NSW 2018, Australia.

Order No. AM987954
ISBN 1-84609-798-3
This book © Copyright 2006 Wise Publications,
a division of Music Sales Limited.

Unauthorised reproduction of any part
of this publication by any means including
photocopying is an infringement of copyright.

Printed in the EU.

www.musicsales.com

Your Guarantee of Quality

As publishers, we strive to produce every book
to the highest commercial standards.

The book has been carefully designed
to minimise awkward page turns and to
make playing from it a real pleasure.

Particular care has been given to specifying
acid-free, neutral-sized paper made from pulps
which have not been elemental chlorine bleached.

This pulp is from farmed sustainable forests and
was produced with special regard for the environment.

Throughout, the printing and binding have been
planned to ensure a sturdy, attractive publication
which should give years of enjoyment.

If your copy fails to meet our high standards,
please inform us and we will gladly replace it.

Adagio Cantabile (from 'Pathétique Sonata') Beethoven 6

Air On The G String Bach 4

The Can Can Offenbach 9

Clarinet Concerto (second movement, Adagio) Mozart 10

Duettino Mozart 11

Fantaisie Impromptu Chopin 12

Hallelujah Chorus (from 'The Messiah') Handel 14

Hornpipe (from 'Water Music') Handel 17

Lachrimae Antiquae (Flow My Tears) Dowland 22

Largo (from 'Xerxes') Handel 20

Marche Militaire Schubert 23

Minuet (from 'String Quartet') Boccherini 28

Minuet In G Bach 24

Moonlight Sonata Beethoven 26

Ode To Joy (from 'Symphony No. 9') Beethoven 29

Prélude In E Minor Chopin 30

Prelude No.1 In C Major Bach 32

Sarabande In D Minor Handel 34

Swan Lake (Theme) Tchaikovsky 35

Sleepers Awake Bach 36

'Surprise' Symphony Haydn 40

Symphony No. 40 (Theme) Mozart 38

Air On The G String
Composed by Johann Sebastian Bach

Adagio Cantabile
(from 'Pathétique Sonata')

Composed by Ludwig Van Beethoven

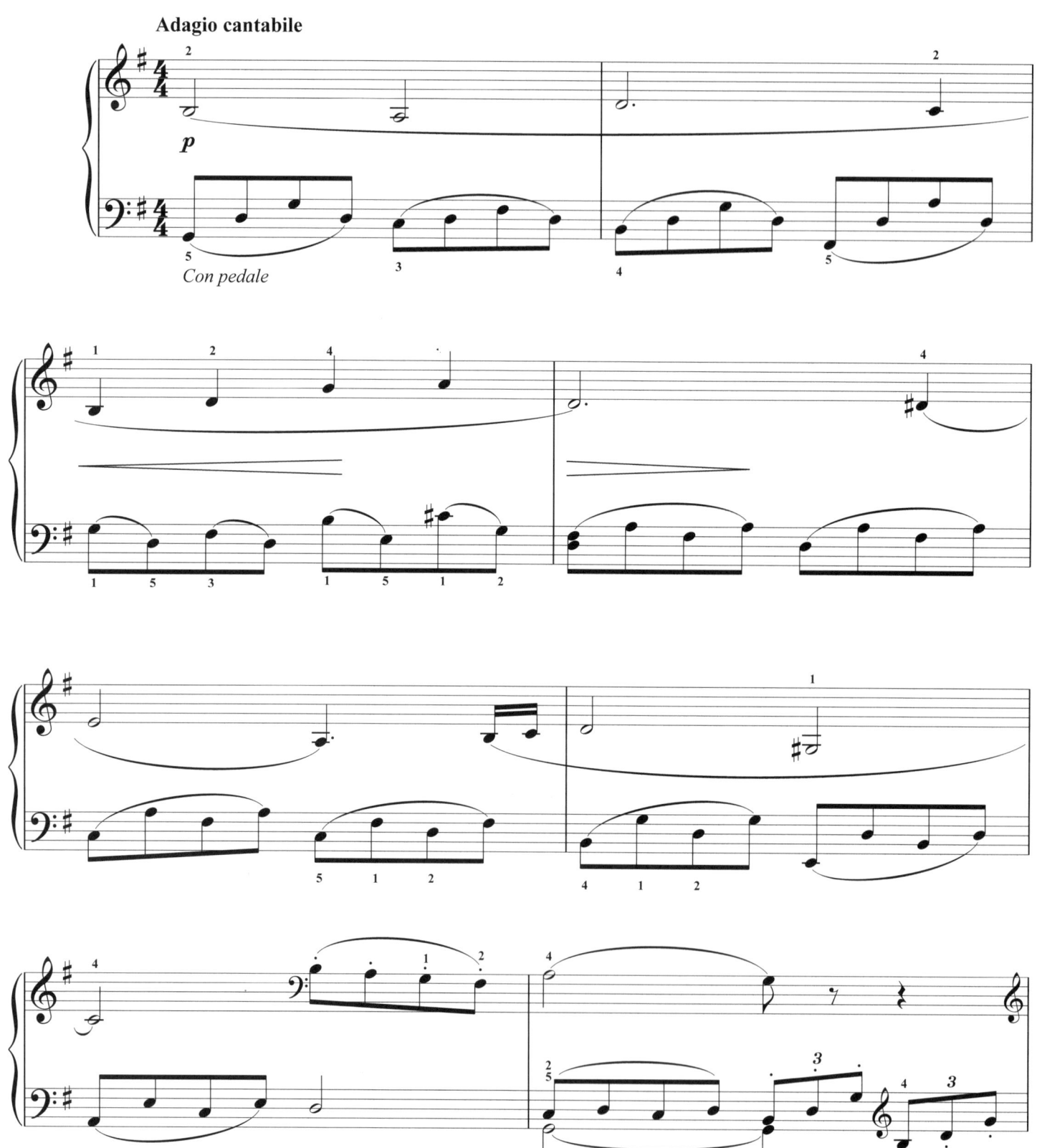

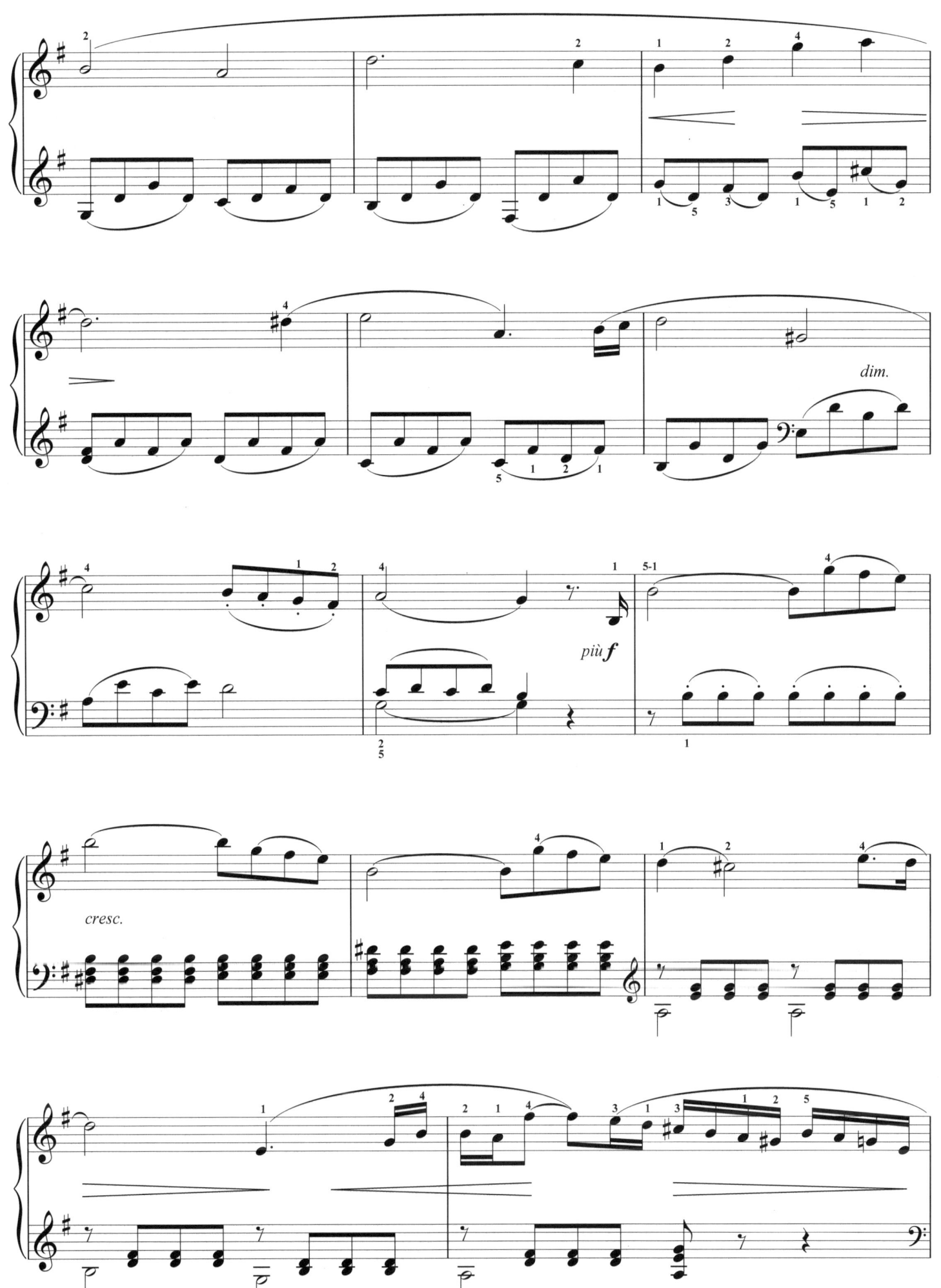

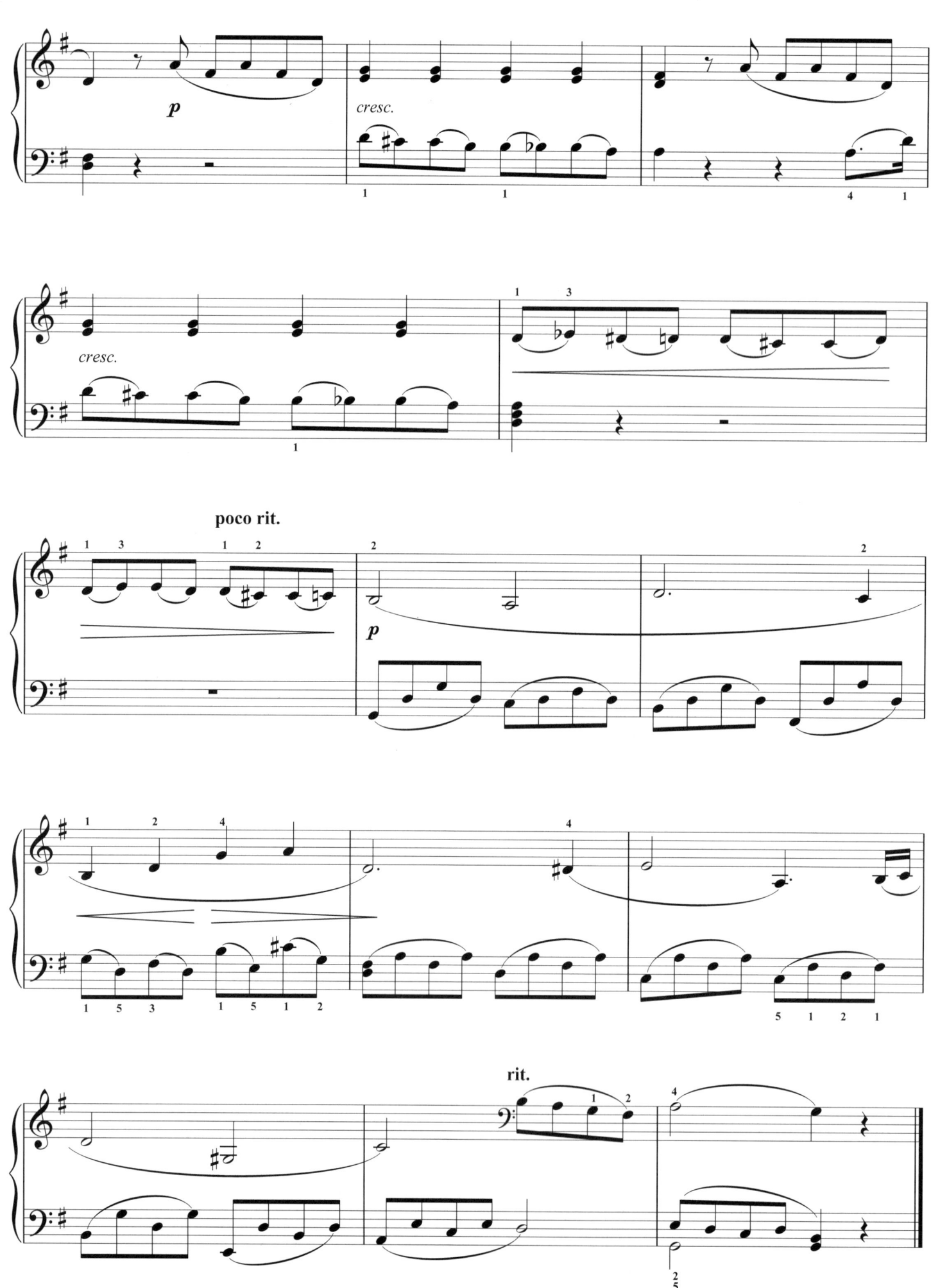

The Can Can

Composed by Jacques Offenbach

Clarinet Concerto
(second movement, Adagio)

Composed by Wolfgang Amadeus Mozart

Duettino

Composed by Wolfgang Amadeus Mozart

Fantaisie Impromptu

Composed by Frédéric Chopin

Smoothly and with feeling

Hallelujah Chorus
(from 'The Messiah')

Composed by George Frideric Handel

Hornpipe
(from 'Water Music')

Composed by George Frideric Handel

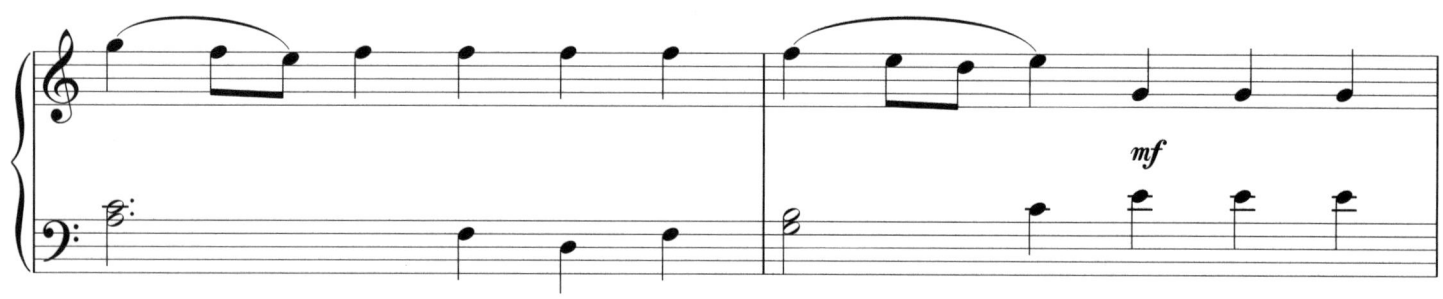
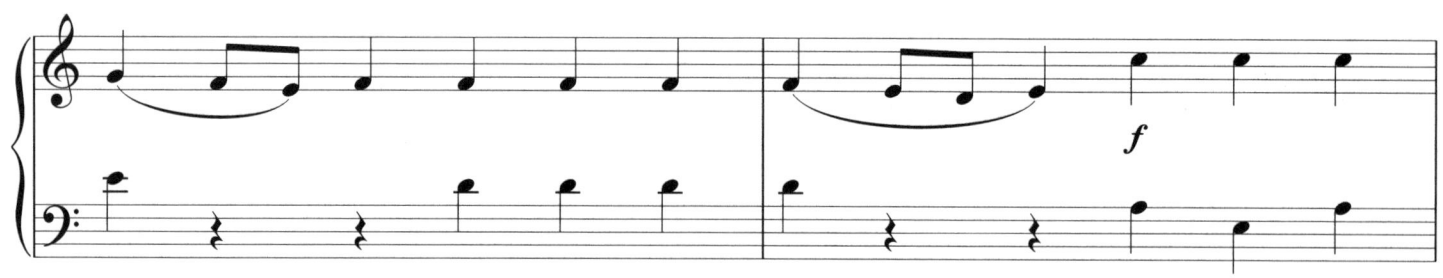

Largo
(from 'Xerxes')

Composed by George Frideric Handel

Lachrimae Antiquae
(Flow My Tears)
Composed by John Dowland

Marche Militaire

Composed by Franz Schubert

Minuet In G

Composed by Johann Sebastian Bach

Allegretto

Moonlight Sonata
Composed by Ludwig Van Beethoven

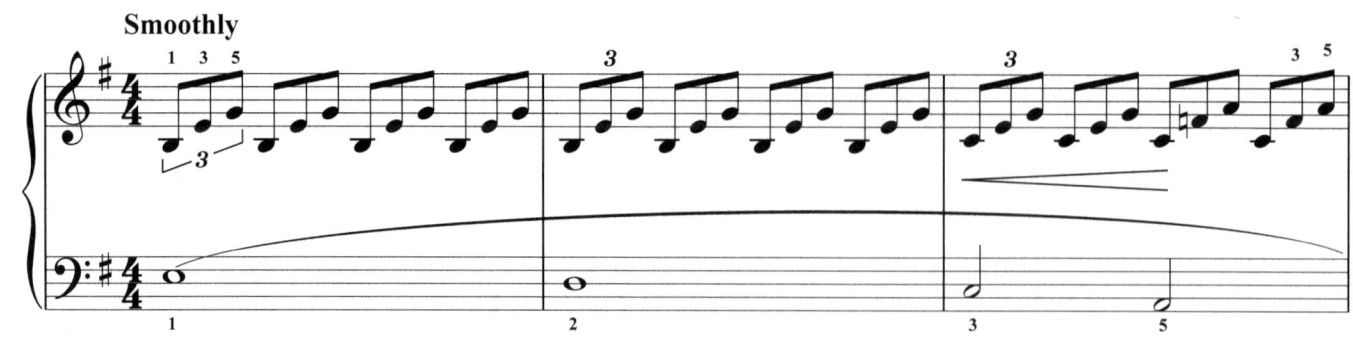
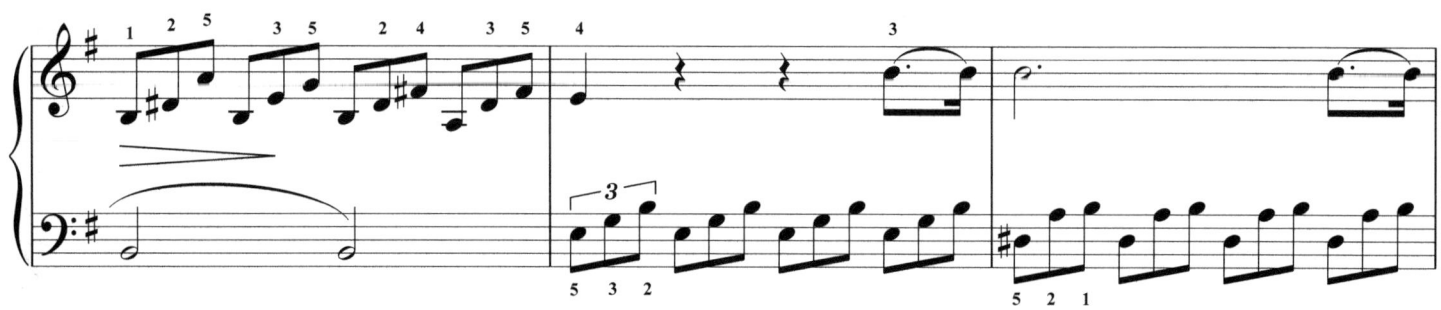

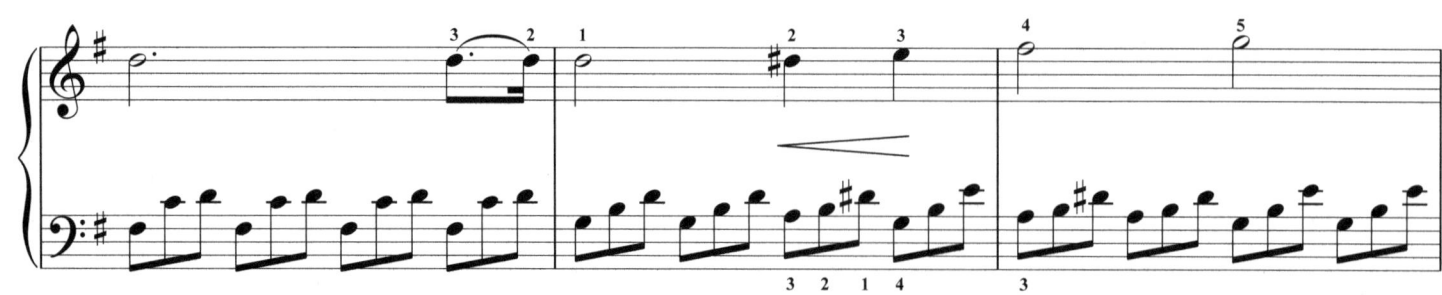

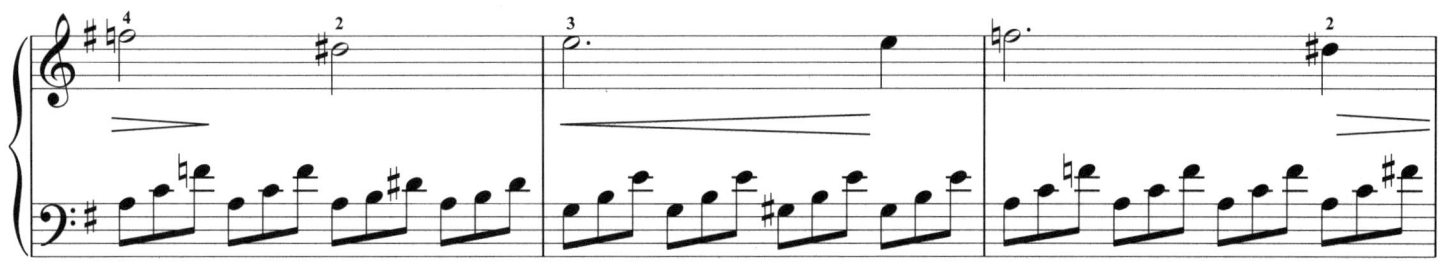
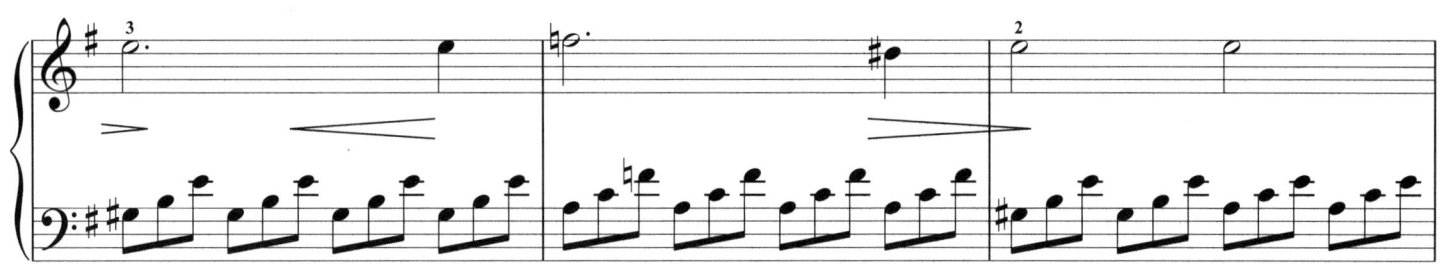
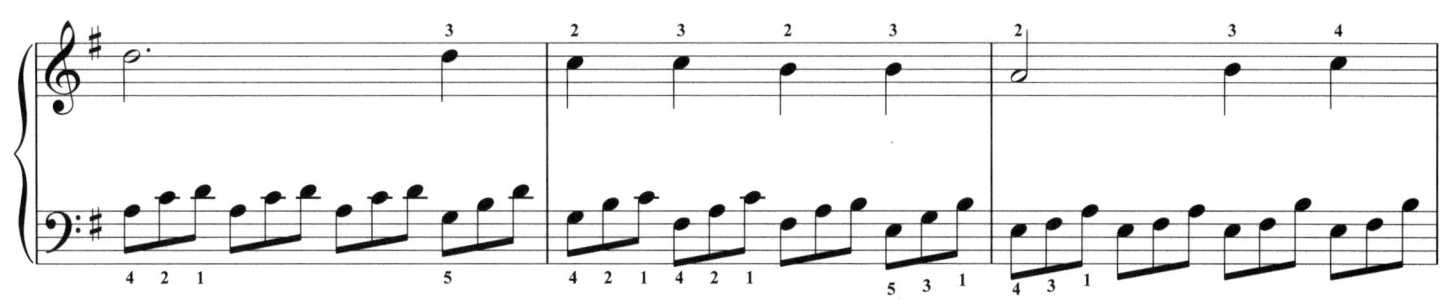

Minuet
(from 'String Quartet')

Composed by Luigi Boccherini

Moderato

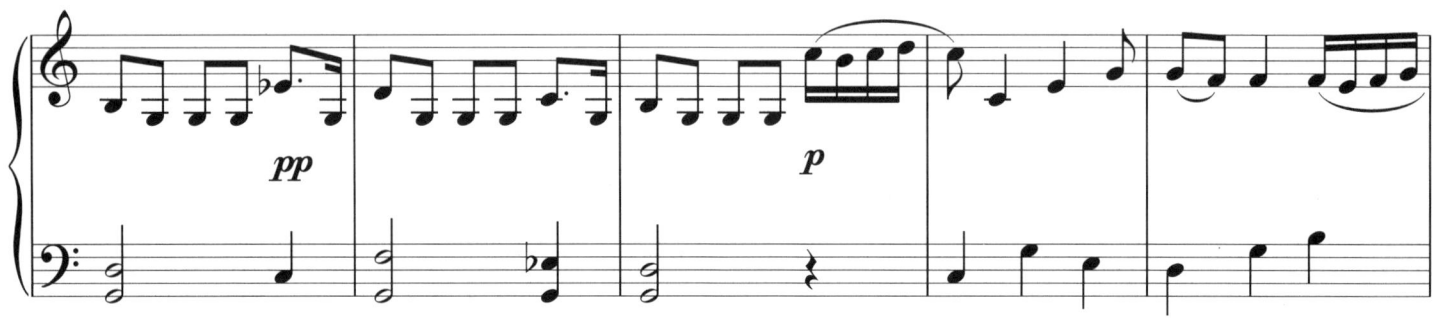

Ode To Joy
(from 'Symphony No. 9')
Composed by Ludwig Van Beethoven

Prélude In E Minor

Composed by Frédéric Chopin

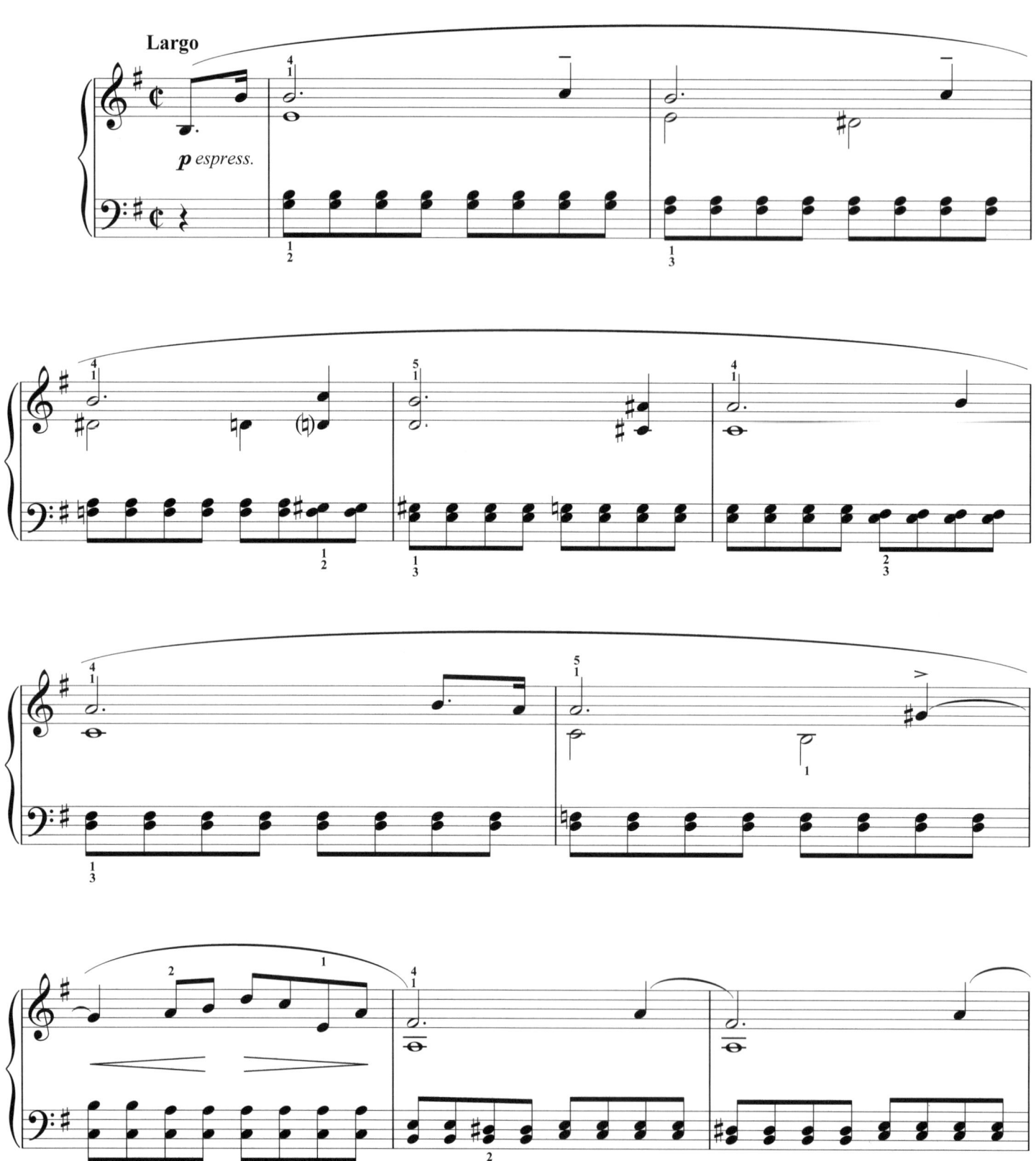

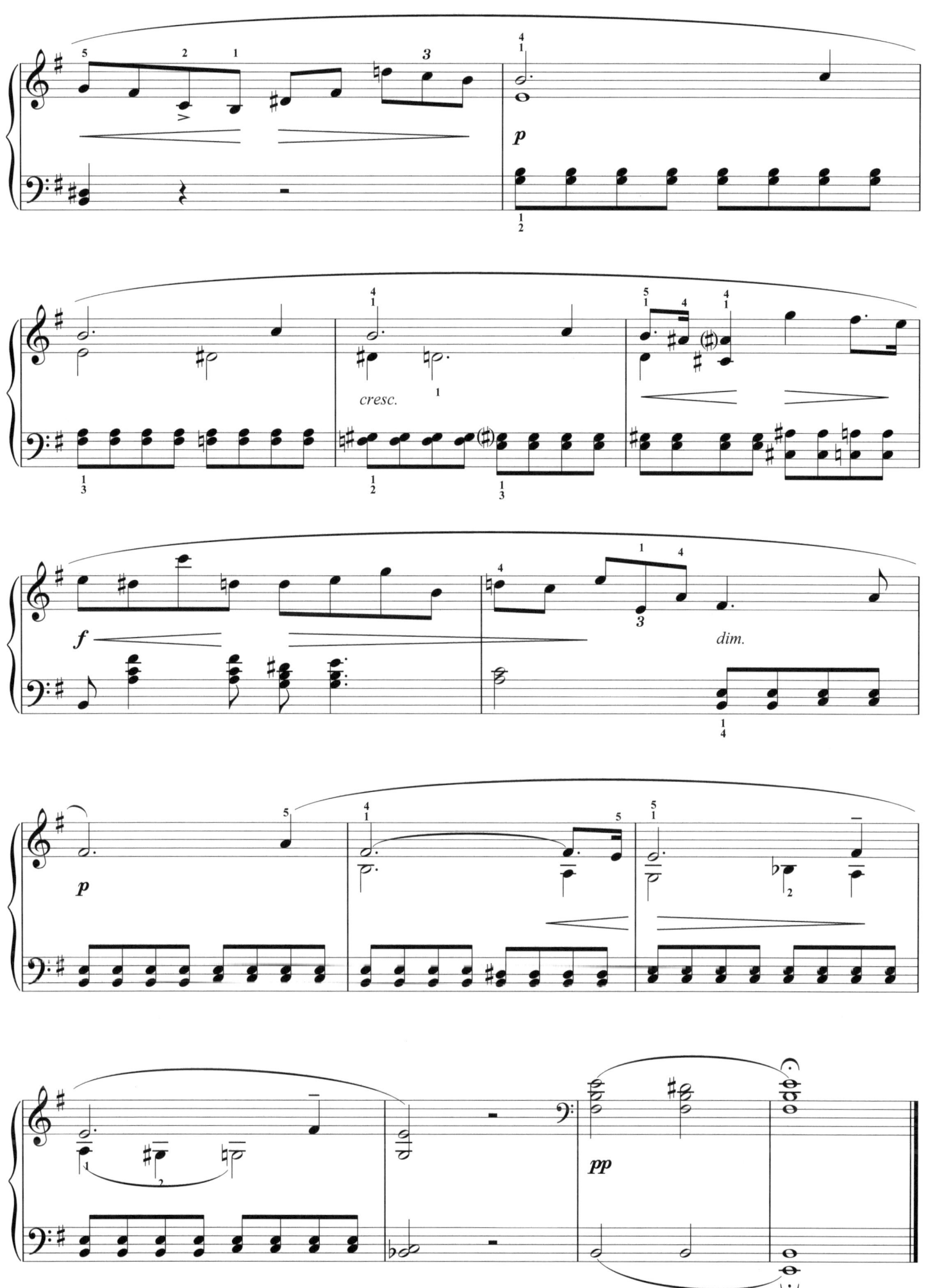

Prelude No. 1 In C Major

Composed by Johann Sebastian Bach

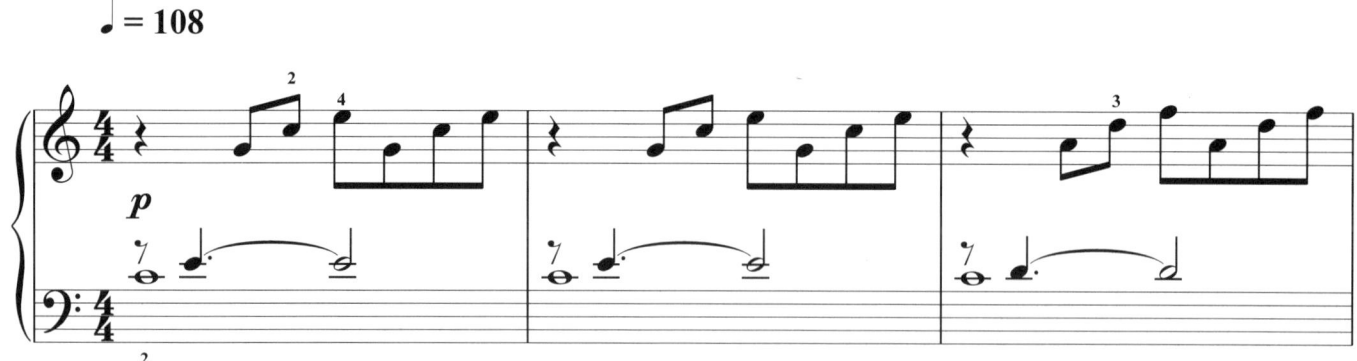

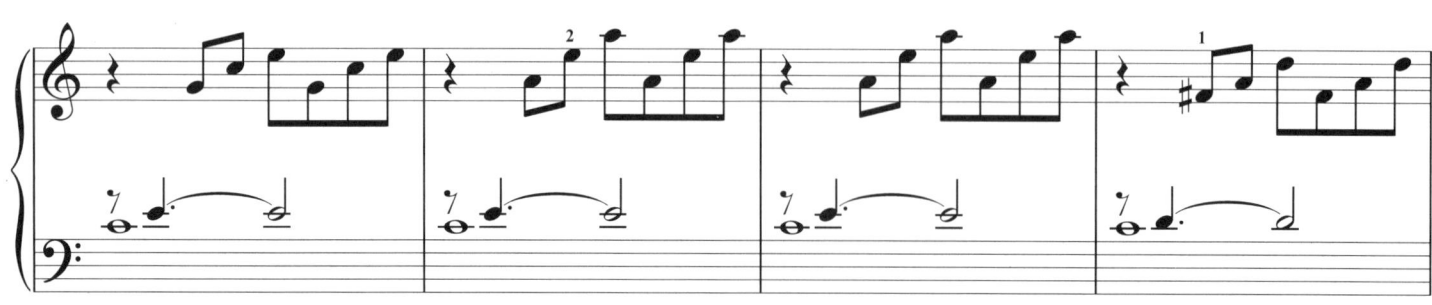
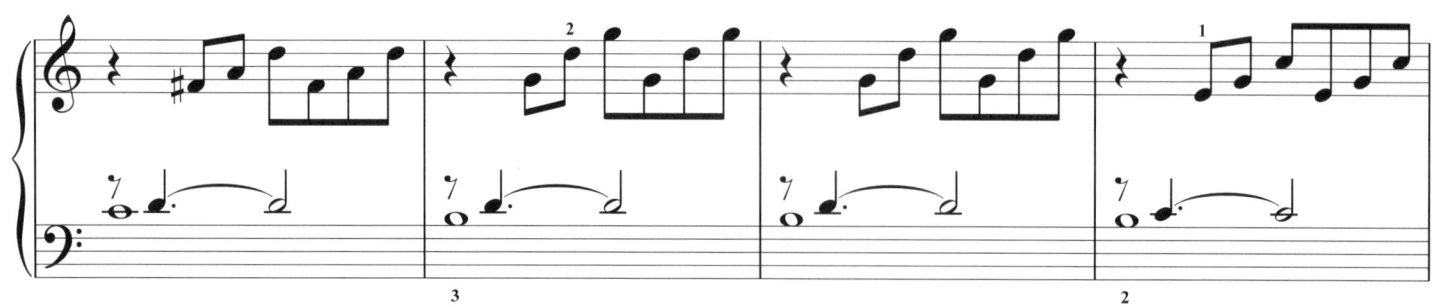

Sarabande In D Minor

Composed by George Frideric Handel

Swan Lake

(Theme)

Composed by Peter Ilyich Tchaikovsky

Andante

Sleepers Awake

Composed by Johann Sebastian Bach

© Copyright 2006 Dorsey Brothers Music Limited.
All Rights Reserved. International Copyright Secured.

Symphony No. 40
(Theme)

Composed by Wolfgang Amadeus Mozart

'Surprise' Symphony

Composed by Josef Haydn

Andante

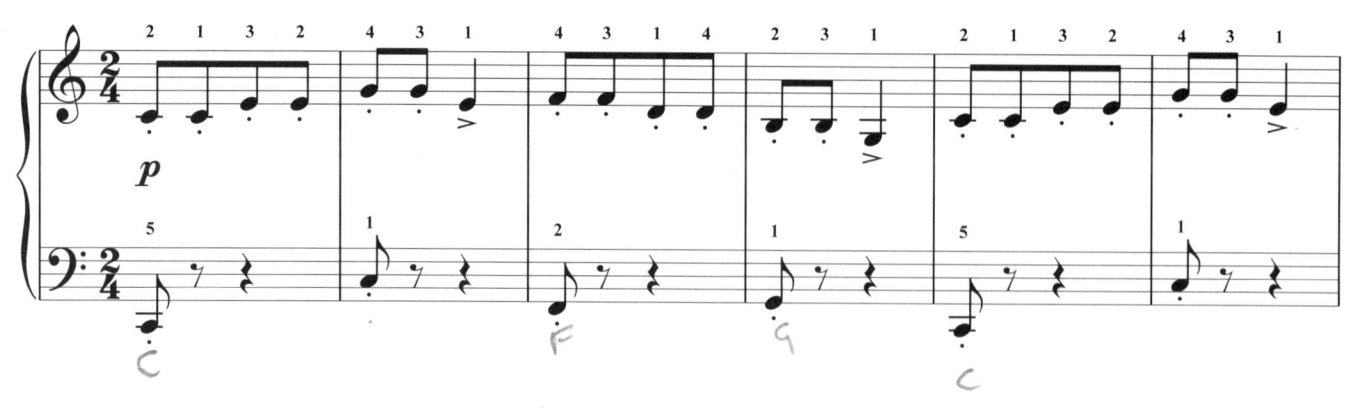

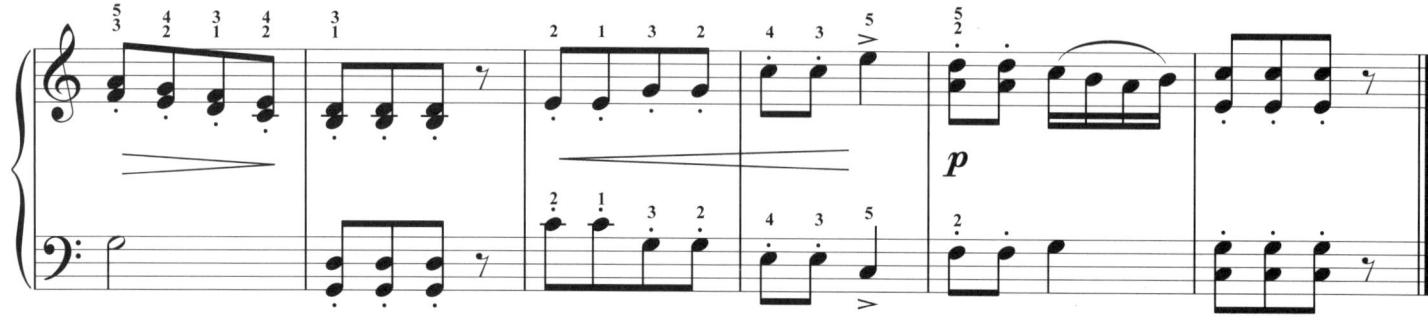